Everybody Ought to Go to Learning Centers

Linda Burba

BAKER BOOK HOUSE
Grand Rapids, Michigan 49506

Copyright 1980 by
Beacon Hill Press of Kansas City

Reprinted 1981 by
Baker Book House
with permission of copyright owner

ISBN: 0-8010-0811-5

Printed in the United States of America

This book is dedicated
to our three sons,
Matthew, Michael, and Mark,
who keep our home
a center of learning.

Acknowledgments

Heartfelt thanks is given to the people who readied me for this book: to Marjorie Kunz, who taught me that it is all right for children to act like children; to Juanita Lutz, who offered help from her successful teaching background in public school and in our local Sunday school; to Ruth Angles and Brenda Brian, who pioneered learning center teaching in our local church; to Linda Borton, who willingly shared her Junior Department experiences; and to Keith, my husband, who encouraged through the entire project.

Contents

Foreword

In recent years, one of the most exciting trends in public education has been the use of individualized learning center activities. Many children who once were bored with school, learning little, have come alive to education. Using a variety of media to learn through creative activity, boys and girls experience the joy of personal discovery.

Christian educators, too, have become excited about the possibility of using learning centers in the Sunday school. They have realized that Bible truths can be taught at centers just as well as reading, math, or language arts. But because most curriculum materials are not written for a total learning center approach, many questions arise. "How do we get started?" "What guidelines for using the centers should we give to the boys and girls?" "Can we adapt our present curriculum materials to a learning center approach?"

Linda Burba has answered all these questions, and more, in this book. She is well qualified to speak authoritatively on the subject. She has used learning centers with children not only in public school but also in the Sunday school. She knows how to organize and carry out a learning center approach, and she shares a wealth of specific activity ideas.

If you have ever considered using learning centers in your Sunday school, this book is just what you are looking for. If you have not, you will find your excitement growing as you study her suggestions. Linda really believes that "everybody ought to go to learning centers." By the time you have finished this book, I feel confident that you will, too.

Miriam J. Hall
Executive Director
Department of Children's Ministries

Chapter 1

The Five Ws of Learning Centers

"I don't mean to be a tattletale, but your boys weren't in their Sunday school class today," a friend sheepishly informed us. My husband and I looked at each other, startled.

As was customary for us, we had arrived 15 or 20 minutes early that day, in time to ready the Teen Department for the opening session. (I must confess these early arrivals are not as much our parental efficiency as our boys' habit patterns. We happen to be blessed with youngsters who awaken us by 7 a.m. or so every morning of the week.) As usual, we had allowed our four-year-old twin boys to help distribute songbooks in the Teen Department, where my husband was department leader. When it was almost time to begin, we had sent them to their own class. We could usually depend on them to go directly there. What had happened today?

Through a quick investigation we learned that the boys had stopped off at the Kindergarten-Primary Department, walked in unabashed, and joined the activities in progress there. The teachers, knowing who they were, decided to let them stay. From then on until they reached the proper age to become regular participants in that department, we had to monitor the boys closely as they passed that open, inviting doorway.

Those two had always enjoyed the nursery class, had had loving and talented teachers, and had always come out with positive feelings. But that other open door remained a temptation.

And no wonder. My husband and I are both educators, and we understand the pull. Inside that open door, learning centers were in operation. Teachers with loving, accepting attitudes supervised enthusiastic children as they expressed eager, creative desires to interact in the learning center setting.

In this book we will attempt to convey the excitement that those two little boys felt in this activity-oriented approach to teaching and learning. We will discuss reasons for the method and also how to implement a change to this kind of teaching. Then, in Chapters 4 and 5, we will outline actual center ideas to help the beginning leader set up and get started.

The main traits needed in leaders chosen to introduce learning center teaching are love for children and an open mind to learn new methods. When the change is complete, open wide the doors of your church, because children will respond!

To Begin . . .

Until recently, teachers in the church setting most often used traditional teaching methods. In this approach the teacher is an authority—speaker, fact-giver, and quizzer. The role of the student is learner, listener, fact-receiver, and respondent. In short, the teacher's role is active; the student's role is passive.

However, too many times the result seems to be that the teacher does, while the student doesn't. For instance, the teacher talks; the student doesn't. The teacher walks around. The student doesn't. The teacher asks questions; the student doesn't.

In academic education, this formula was used for centuries. Then in recent years educators began to wonder what would happen if children were permitted to become more exploratory in their acquisition of knowledge. It seemed to some that there might be a deeper level of understanding if students became actively involved in the learning process. A Chinese proverb states that concept in this way:

> *I hear, and I forget;*
> *I see, and I remember;*
> *I do, and I understand.*

Progressive educators decided to find out if "doing" did correlate with "understanding." Thus activity-oriented learning evolved. In this learning approach children are doers, not just passive participants. This new philosophy became known as open education. Not only was the teacher-student relationship altered, but teaching methods and classroom settings also took on a less rigid form. This helped to create a feeling of exploration—a certain freedom for the student to explore, to question, to test his own academic limits. The needs of the individual student became paramount. Lee Smith states, "Each individual needs physical activity; he needs to talk; he needs to be a part of a small group; he needs time to work alone; he needs creative activities; he needs some large group experiences; he needs to be himself."[1]

Learning center education provides opportunities for these kinds of activities. Centers are selected in the church setting to accentuate and/or amplify curriculum unit concepts. They provide opportunity for each child to extend his knowledge or apply it in a different way, thus

---

1. From the book by Lee L. Smith, *Jack out of the Box* (Nyack, N.Y.: Parker Publishing Company, Inc., 1974).

reinforcing what he has learned or encouraging him to acquire additional understanding.

But that all sounds so theoretical. How does it really work? In theory, active, talkative, exploring children are eager to learn. But anyone who has worked with children of any age knows that there must be limits to the activity and to the noise level of talking. There must be guidelines to help the teacher know what to expect of exploratory learning. Fear of pandemonium prevents some adults from ever letting go of the traditional authoritarian classroom setup.

Learning center education does give the student more freedom of activity, but it does not mean that there are no restraints on behavior. On the contrary, students function better after knowing the expectations and limits of each activity. There will be more talking and movement than in the traditional classroom, since each pupil is encouraged to be creative and expressive. Nevertheless, this need not be frightening nor appear as lack of control.

The teacher may speak softly to an individual who is talking loudly. "Let's use our indoor voices," can be suggested to a young child. The older child can be reminded, "Remember to talk quietly." Positive statements such as these generally produce positive results. Those who have tried learning centers find that the teacher's calm manner and tolerant attitude influences the noise level. Also, the noise level diminishes slowly but steadily as the open approach to teaching becomes normal procedure to the class.

With these ideas in mind, let us examine the learning center method of teaching.

What Are Learning Centers?

What exactly are learning centers? (They are sometimes called interest centers. Both terms will be used in this book.) Simply stated, a learning center is a separate location of learning. The learning is determined, in part, by the individual interest of the student. Thus, the term *learning center* designates a physical setting with a particular kind of activity which teaches, reinforces, or applies an idea, concept, or fact to the student.

For instance, in a lesson on the story of Jesus and the lad's loaves and fishes, there might be one center for making the kind of bread used in Bible times. Another center might contain small loaves of bread for the children to see how many pieces they could tear off. This would help them realize the miracle which had to be performed to feed so many people until they were full. A third center could provide crayons and paper where interested youngsters would draw some phase of the story. There might also be a dress-up center for younger children to act out the story in costume, and a workbook center where children would answer questions regarding the story.

Chapters 4 and 5 give specific ideas for centers which can be adapted to complement curriculum.

Why Have Learning Centers?

The answer to the "why?" of learning centers is found in the needs of the child.

The activity-oriented nature of such centers allows more freedom for the students and requires a higher level of tolerance and patience from teachers. As mentioned earlier, this attitude of tolerance is not the same as unrestricted permissiveness which leads to chaotic behavior by the class. Rather, it should be viewed as allowing normal social and emotional behavior for a particular age-group, within the confines of the limits of expected behavior spelled out to the group and to individuals as the need arises. The amount of cooperation, responsibility, and self-control expected from third graders, for example, will differ from that expected from nursery children. Once teachers master this accepting attitude, the needs of the child can be met.

First, there are intellectual and instructional needs. These vary with the individual, but in interest center teaching the child paces himself.

Second, the child's social needs are met as he mingles with others, shares, gives, receives, and works out differences. What better place could there be to learn proper attitudes! Acceptance of one another, lack of competition in the individual learning situations, and bettering one's own skills in cooperation with others are positive by-products of such an approach.

Third, the child's emotional needs can be met more easily in the open setting. Children are allowed to engage in activities which facilitate expression of various emotions. The observant teacher loves the child through both positive and negative emotions, thus modeling New Testament, Christ-taught, unconditional love. Also, the child can be encouraged to develop in this type of atmosphere.

Fourth, the child can express his creative needs in learning centers. In an interest center setting, each student is encouraged to achieve what he wishes to produce with his particular abilities and creative desires. A teacher, Helen Buckley, poignantly illustrates this with her story entitled "The Little Boy."

> Once a little boy went to school.
> He was quite a little boy.
> And it was quite a big school.
> But when the little boy
> Found that he could go to his room
> By walking right in from the door outside,
> He was happy,
> And the school did not seem
> Quite so big anymore.

One morning,
When the little boy had been in school awhile,
The teacher said:
"Today we are going to make a picture."
"Good!" thought the little boy.
He liked to make pictures.
He could make all kinds:
Lions and tigers,
Chickens and cows,
Trains and boats—
And he took out his box of crayons
And began to draw.

But the teacher said, "Wait!
It is not time to begin!"
And she waited until everyone looked ready.
"Now," said the teacher,
"We are going to make flowers."
"Good!" thought the little boy.
He liked to make flowers,
And he began to make beautiful ones
With his pink and orange and blue crayons.

But the teacher said, "Wait!
And I will show you how."
And she drew a flower on the blackboard.
And it was red, with a green stem.
"There," said the teacher.
"Now you may begin."

The little boy looked at the teacher's flower.
Then he looked at his own flower.
He liked his flower better than the teacher's.
But he did not say this.
He just turned his paper over
And made a flower like the teacher's.
It was red, with a green stem.

On another day,
When the little boy had opened
The door from the outside all by himself,
The teacher said:
"Today we are going to make something with clay."

"Good!" thought the little boy.
He liked clay.
He could make all kinds of things with clay:
Snakes and snowmen,
Elephants and mice,
Cars and trucks—
And he began to pull and pinch
His ball of clay.
But the teacher said:
"Wait! It is not time to begin."
And she waited until everyone looked ready.

"Now," said the teacher,
"We are going to make a dish."
"Good!" thought the little boy.
He liked to make dishes,
And he began to make some
That were all shapes and sizes.

The teacher said, "Wait!
And I will show you how."
And she showed everyone how to make
One deep dish.
"There," said the teacher,
"Now you may begin."
The little boy looked at the teacher's dish.
Then he looked at his own.
He liked his dishes better than the teacher's.
But he did not say this.
He just rolled his clay into a big ball again
And made a dish like the teacher's.
It was a deep dish.

And pretty soon
The little boy learned to wait.
And to watch,
And to make things just like the teacher.
And pretty soon
He didn't make things of his own anymore.
Then it happened
That the little boy and his family
Moved to another house,
In another city,

And the little boy
Had to go to another school.

This school was even bigger
Than this other one,
And there was no door from the outside
Into his room.
He had to go up some big steps,
And walk down a long hall
To get to his room.
And the very first day
He was there,
The teacher said:
"Today we are going to make a picture."
"Good!" thought the little boy,
And he waited for the teacher
To tell him what to do.
But the teacher didn't say anything;
She just walked around the room.

When she came to the little boy
She said, "Don't you want to make a picture?"
"Yes," said the little boy.
"What are we going to make?"
"I don't know until you make it," said the teacher.
"How shall I make it?" asked the little boy.
"Why, any way you like," said the teacher.
"And any color?" asked the little boy.
"Any color," said the teacher.
"If everyone made the same picture, and used the same
        colors,
How would I know who made what,
And which was which?"
"I don't know," said the little boy.
And he began to make pink and orange and blue flowers.

He liked his new school
Even if it didn't have a door
Right in from the outside!

Reprinted with permission of *School Arts* magazine and Helen
Buckley Simkewicz.

An interest center teacher would encourage as the second teacher did. She would talk about how beautiful the flowers were. Any sincere work effort made by a child of any age should be appreciated for just that—sincere effort. Within such a positive environment, children most often will strive to improve, even to excel, knowing that whatever they attempt will be accepted. This knowledge lessens the fear of failure, which is why so many children refuse to try.

Where Are Learning Centers Found?

Learning centers may be found anywhere there is an educational endeavor. In public education, they are found everywhere from preschool through the secondary school. Of course, as children grow older, the types of centers become more refined and often more academic, with less emphasis on enjoyment and more on knowledge.

In the church setting, learning centers can be utilized in Sunday school, children's church, Caravan, children's missionary chapters, Sunday evening worship, and during adult midweek programs. This type of teaching can be utilized in any size church. Large churches, with more space, may use centers in departments where children of only one or two grades meet. Smaller churches can combine three or four grade levels successfully (K-3, 4-6), depending on the number of children in each age category and the type of group.

The important thing to remember is that interest centers can be used in any church setting, large or small.

Who Is Involved?

We have discussed briefly the importance of the teacher's attitude of accepting the normal, expected behavior for the child, at his age level. Beyond this, the teacher using learning centers should possess these qualities:

1. Function in a supportive role. The student's activity is of central importance. The teacher reinforces and encourages.

2. Express keen interest in what is happening with each individual.

3. Show enthusiasm with every work effort the child makes.

4. Respect each student as an individual. The child is expected to achieve only up to his own potential. Never compare one pupil's work with another's superior or inferior product. The teacher must remember never to confuse age with ability.

5. Assist as a helper, rather than being the never-wrong leader. The teacher *participates* in instruction and in the learning process; he does not just give directions.

What then is the pupil's role? As expressed earlier, the child is an active participant. He becomes a doer, not just a receiver of information. A certain amount of independence is expected in the learning experiences at interest centers.

Older children may be involved in an evaluation process after the program has been in progress for a time. Ask responsible youngsters (individually) what activities they want more of, less of. In formulating questions to find out likes and dislikes, emphasize the positive aspect of what they have learned in the centers.

Another important observation about learning centers is that centers for nursery, kindergarten, and primary children (grades 1 and 2) need to focus more on manipulative materials. Especially nursery children function best with concrete facts. Ideas and theories need to be related to things they can experience through their senses. Chapters

4 and 5 describe interest centers appropriate for these young minds.

Middlers (grades 3 and 4) and juniors (grades 5 and 6) have developed more cognitive skills and enjoy being challenged to use their academic ability. For instance, they can learn through their own research and sharing. Challenge is often the answer to disinterest in these grades. Suggestions for those ages also are contained in Chapters 4 and 5.

When Shall We Begin?

Learning center users have found that the best time to introduce such a program is at the beginning of a new quarter, to coincide with printed materials. In the fall, when students are enthusiastic about a new school year, may be the ideal time of year to change to the center approach. The materials in the children's activity packets for Sunday school, provided by your publishing house, can be adapted to interest center teaching. As soon as the upcoming quarter's packet arrives, the supervisor and teachers should take ample time to study and adapt the material to center use.

For instance, a Bible story may be acted out in a drama dress-up center. Puppets may be used to tell a contemporary story in the puppet-making center. For older children, Bible facts from the activity book or Bible story can be used in a game center. Also, teachers may supplement the curriculum unit theme with ideas from this book and other sources, such as elementary school activity books, game books, and so on.

Steps for getting church authorities to approve a change to learning center teaching are outlined in Chapter 2. However, one word of caution is appropriate here. Introduce the program gradually. Especially where there is resistance to change, use one or two simple interest centers as a supplement to the regular program. Then, after teachers and students in the department have become adjusted to the new system of operation, a complete program can be built around the interest center approach. Schedule suggestions for such a program are outlined in Chapter 3.

Now How Do We Begin?

That's what this book is all about! Read on—absorb —pray—then do! Learning center teaching will be successful in your church if everyone involved practices the attitudes of cooperation, tolerance, patience, willingness to learn, and responsibility—and mixes them with the most important factor, "lots o' love."

Chapter 2

Ready or Not

There are five major steps in making the change from traditional teaching to activity-oriented learning center teaching. It is important that the channels of authority in your church organization be followed. Adapt these five steps as needed.

Step 1: Talk with the pastor as soon as you have developed the initial proposal. This should be done before all the details are worked out. The department supervisor, or the person in charge of the group where you want to introduce learning centers, and the director of children's ministries in the local church must agree that such a change is desirable. They then need to make an appointment with the pastor to discuss the pros and cons of the proposed change. Be ready to answer questions about possible changes in room location, addition of equipment, changes in staff, increase in budget, and so on.

Since the new program will require the pastor's approval and reinforcement, he needs to be informed as fully as he desires to be. Knowing what plans are being made makes his job of encouragement easier and enables him to show enthusiasm for the program when it is presented to the board, or committee, responsible for Christian education in the church. Most pastors are eager to give their support to a well-thought-out program that results in more effective teaching of the Bible.

Step 2: Present the proposal to the board, or committee, which has jurisdiction in your church structure. Make sure the pastor is present at the meeting when you do this.

Since the most common educational unit in the church is the Sunday school, consider what kinds of information you need in your presentation to the board or committee.

a. Approach the meeting with a positive attitude and with enthusiasm. Challenge them to try a new approach to teaching.

b. Inform them about students in the group where you want to make the change and how it will help them to learn the Bible more effectively.

c. Be honest about the problems you may confront. Don't discuss, or even mention, specific children with whom you may have had behavior difficulties in the past. This protects the child's reputation and leaves room for him to improve his behavior in the future. However, do be realistic in your evaluation as to how this new approach may affect problems that have risen in the past.

In addition to questions on discipline, the board may wish to know how the new setup will affect the janitorial services. Assure them that normal cleanup will be taken care of by the department, just as it has been in the past. Also, children will be encouraged to tidy their work areas.

d. Inform the board about the teachers you have in mind for the department. Stress the individualized attention that will be given to the children. Point out that in a supportive role, teachers will be better able to draw out the reluctant or shy child and to guide the recalcitrant one.

e. Have ready a detailed plan to show how and when you intend to begin the learning center approach. Remember that a gradual change, with much communication on what is happening between students, teachers, and parents, will make the transition more smooth. Imagine the insecure feelings which would surface if the supervisor announced that a new way of conducting class activities would begin in two weeks.

Once assured that the interest center approach is not only superior to the current one, but exciting as well, the board's decision will surely be, "Permission granted. Proceed."

Step 3: The third step is perhaps the most crucial in the success or failure of the program—enlisting the enthusiastic support and cooperation of the teachers.

The decision to change to learning center teaching must be accepted by the teachers involved. Call a departmental planning meeting and present the plan. Ask teachers to cooperate and challenge them to be open to change. If any are unwilling to participate, they probably will ask to resign. Do not try to coerce them to remain. Unresponsive teachers could hamper the success of the new program. Give teachers who are a bit reluctant, but who want to remain in the department, the more structured centers, such as workbook activities and memory work projects, where they will feel more comfortable.

After willing helpers have committed themselves, explain exactly what changes will be taking place. Explain that the open feeling of the new situation and the increased freedom of movement will undoubtedly produce a higher noise level than that to which they are presently accustomed. Assure them that this is to be expected and, though the children will be encouraged from time to time to speak in softer voices, noise is not bad *if* it comes out of excitement for the creative adventures the children are exploring. Veterans of interest center teaching report that the noise level will decrease gradually as everyone becomes adjusted to the new way of doing things.

Another common early experience that teachers may be told to expect is that children will tend to "hop" from center to center when they are permitted to choose centers. They seem to want to be sure not to miss anything at first. After the breaking-in period, this pattern of behavior is modified also. The child then will find one, or perhaps two, centers which hold his interest for most of the session, even when a flexible schedule is provided.

At this meeting explain and discuss the supportive role of the teacher. Teachers should understand that they will not be merely bystanders to the educational process. Rather, they will be active in the planning process and be interested helpers when a student needs aid or information. Also, another essential role the teacher fills is to express enthusiasm for every work effort of the child.

Step 4: Successful implementation of a changed approach to teaching requires pleased parents. Even in a superior educational situation, unsupportive parents can undermine the enthusiasm of the students and the morale of the teaching staff.

To encourage positive parental input, arrange an explanatory in-service meeting for all parents of the children affected by the program. Presenting details of the plan with an enthusiastic spirit will lessen fears that a proposed change of current structure sometimes produces.

Some parents may ask, "What will my child learn?" Assure them that children will be learning the same curriculum content as in the past. It is just the method of teaching that knowledge that will be altered. The traditional approach will be replaced with a "learning-can-be-fun-and-interesting" approach.

Let parents know they are welcome to come into the

meeting place to observe after the program is established. Another good idea is to schedule open house. Parents whose last names begin with certain letters of the alphabet may come on a designated Sunday. This allows parents opportunity to view interest centers in operation—and they should be encouraged to participate in the centers with their own youngsters.

Keep parents informed of the program's progress through letters, phone calls, quarterly parent meetings, and personal contact. This assures the parents that the teachers truly are interested in each particular child, and the parents find it easier to support creative change. In addition, they also become more actively involved in their child's learning, and the home can better complement the religious educational process of the church.

Ready or Not—Here We Come!

Step 5: In all of the above preparation, the students are not involved. However, support by the pastor, approval from the board in charge, cooperative teachers, and enthusiastic parents are all secondary to vital persons in this activity-oriented teaching—the children.

Getting ready for the changeover is much less complicated for the pupils than for the adults. In the home, parents find that most young children adapt to change much faster and easier than older persons. However, a move to a new home, a new school, or a new church is facilitated by the knowledge and assurance that the love and care of parents is constant. A similar approach should be used by understanding teachers as the time for using the new teaching method approaches.

About two weeks in advance, teachers should give early elementary students a small amount of information about what is going to happen soon. Assure these young children that the "big people" will be there to explain to them what to do. Emphasize the staff's excitement and attitude of anticipation. Most children will mirror the attitude of teachers who have gained their respect as being trustworthy.

Preschool children need less warning of change, except that the room will look different. At this age impact of change will occur after they arrive for the first session. Teachers should allow the children to explore the room freely to familiarize themselves with the new environment.

Older children should be given more detail regarding what to expect. A discussion of positive behavior expectations will be effective at this point of preparation. Students should be advised that the new system will be a more active way of learning, but that there will be limits to where they can go and what they can do. Stress the challenge of working at their own rate and the increased opportunity to be creative and independent.

A positive, enthusiastic spirit on the teacher's part is imperative in preparing the children for change. Once this contagious feeling has caught on, teachers will be delighted as the excited children look forward to the opening of the door, eager to begin learning Christian principles at attractive, challenging, and meaningful learning centers.

Chapter 3

Let's Get Organized

Some persons are convinced that learning centers would be an effective method of teaching but feel their church lacks physical facilities to use them. This is a false assumption. Present facilities, whatever they may be, can be adapted to provide for learning center teaching.

What Kind of Room Do We Need?

The ideal room for the interest center approach to teaching is large, with space enough to house all, or at least most, of the centers used in any one teaching session. It may be set up in this way:

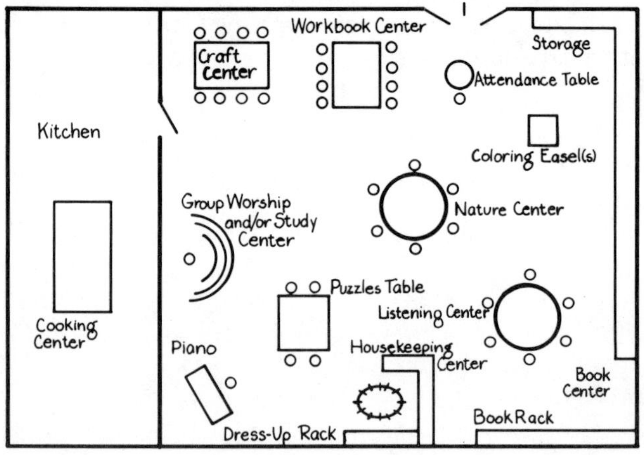

Some large meeting rooms have adjacent smaller-sized classrooms. Divide the large room into a group meeting area and as many center areas as space allows. Locate centers in the adjacent rooms, so that hall traffic will be minimized. These smaller rooms are particularly useful for filmstrip use and for woodworking activities. Here is how an area organized in this way would appear.

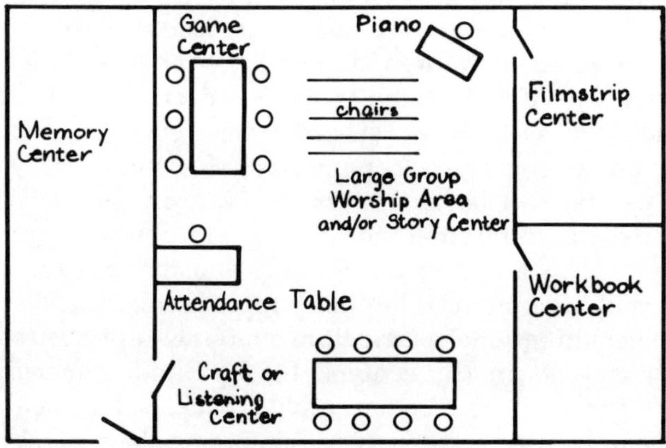

If more than one large room is available when you are choosing a location, consider availability of rest rooms, water for craft use and drinking, electrical outlets for record players, tape recorders, and other audiovisual equipment, and storage space for supplies.

If the only rooms available are so small they hold only one center each, wide hallways may be put to use for small groups of four or five children. Caution must be employed here, though, to use only hallways which allow ample room for passing walkers. Otherwise, this could become a fire hazard. Also, these centers will have to be mobile since they will have to be dismantled and stored elsewhere after use.

What Materials Will We Use?

"We have the room, but what special materials will we need for this program?" one may ask. "Our budget is limited. Besides, we already have the denominational curriculum materials. How can we use those?"

Again, the answer to these questions is in adaptability. No expensive special materials are needed to begin learning center teaching. Common, easily available, and inexpensive materials are the most desirable for center use. For younger children, manipulative objects have high priority. Specific ideas and examples are given in Chapters 4 and 5. Previously purchased items, such as scissors, glue, paste, construction paper, drawing paper, crayons, and paints, will be put to frequent use in this activity-oriented teaching method. Since additional suggested supplies utilize household discards and inexpensive articles, the dilemma of a limited budget is minimized.

Denominational curriculum materials are desired as teaching tools in the centers. In the Sunday school, as previously mentioned, the activity packets for each age level can be used effectively in reinforcing the central unit and lesson theme. For each age, there should also be a workbook or activity book center each session to reinforce the Bible story and/or Christian living concept for that particular day. Children's church packets also contain story ideas that can be acted out, scriptures to use for a Bible game center, and other useful materials.

Curriculum materials are as essential as in the former traditional setup. Simply take the unit and/or session theme to be taught and apply it to center ideas, such as those contained in this book.

Programs other than Sunday school and children's church may also use provided curriculum concepts and then increase student understanding by using center ideas such as those in Chapters 4 and 5.

How Is a Typical Session Conducted?

Sample Procedure for Younger Children
(Preschool Through Grade 4)

The following procedure is suggested for younger children. With adaptations for needs and differences, this may be used for nursery age through fourth grades, depending on the maturity and interest of the older age-groups.

1. Arrival Time

Teachers warmly greet children at the door of the central meeting place.

Take offering as children arrive.

Have a person who knows most of the children mark attendance. If an attendance device is used, assist children in marking their presence.

Give visitors and prospective members a name tag so teachers can address them by name. This avoids the problem of a quiet child becoming overlooked in the larger group setting. It also aids the center helper in knowing which child is new so he can be given special attention until he feels more at home.

If funds are available, a small gift may be given to each new student. Your denominational publishing house catalog will have many inexpensive items, such as combs, pencils, and badges.

2. Presession Activities

Allow children to explore the areas set up for the day. Teachers should encourage them to look, and may explain what they will do at each center when the time comes. One or two centers should be available for the early arrivers to work in, such as a coloring easel, a book table, and/or a listening center.

31

3. Starting Time

At time to begin, call the children together for an opening. This may be designated as "rug meeting" or "share time." Meeting together helps the child feel a sense of belonging to the total group. Establish a signal for calling the children together. For instance, the pianist may softly play the same song each session to let children know that it is time to begin.

4. Opening

As children respond to the call to begin, help them arrange themselves in a semicircle around the teacher in charge. Rows need not be rigid. Young children enjoy sitting on the floor if the area is carpeted. For middlers, be guided by the maturity level of the children. Set up chairs if the children seem to prefer them to sitting on the floor.

All teachers whose centers are already set up should sit among the children—some in the middle of the group. This facilitates a feeling of oneness between staff and children. Also, group order is easier to maintain when a nearby adult can gently remind a restless child to remember to talk quietly.

When you have gained the attention of the students, open with happy observations such as: "My, aren't you a happy-looking group this morning!" Or, "I'm so glad you are all here today. It's so dreary-looking outside that your smiling faces make me happy on the inside!" Or, "You all look so eager to learn today! I'm so glad you've come to learn more about Jesus [or whatever the unit theme is]!"

Such positive input from the teacher at the beginning of the hour encourages positive output from the pupil in his learning activities. The teacher may also ask for volunteers to tell something they are happy about that day.

After the opening observations and sharing time, sing

a few familiar songs. Then present any new ones. Teachers' manuals often contain new songs that correlate with the session or unit concept. Take time to teach these to the children. One interesting way to do this is to record on a cassette tape a few children singing the new song. Later other children may use the tape to learn the song at a listening center.

If someone in the church is talented with poetic ability, ask him to write new words to fit a familiar tune, using lyrics that carry out the theme of the day.

Puppets may share in the opening comments and song time.

Ask a child to pray, if one feels comfortable in doing so, then have an adult pray a short prayer of thanksgiving.

Opening time may also be used to review memory verses. Very young children do this best en masse. Older ones like to say the verses alone. Be sure to use different children from session to session. Some aggressive, bright students will always be eager to participate, but leaders need to encourage the less outgoing ones to contribute from time to time.

Next, tell the Bible story or other curriculum story. Before beginning have the children stand up for a quick stretching exercise to release pent-up energy. This will make it easier for them to sit quietly for the story.

Helpers may rotate in telling the story, unless one individual has the desire and ability to do it every time. Encourage the use of visual aids, such as *Nu-Vu,* and illustrative objects. Young children enjoy dressing up to help dramatize the story. The storyteller or an assistant will have to help with the actions, but professionalism is not the goal; understanding by doing is. Remember to use only two or three children at a time for any activity during the opening. Using too many children who require specific directions leads to group confusion.

Another group activity which fits in well during the opening is *scripture memorization.* Following are several suggestions for learning the memory verse. Ideas *a, c* and *d* can be used for nonreaders; *b* and *e* require reading skills.

a. Puzzle. Print the verse on a large sheet of paper. Cut the words apart, using jagged lines. (See fig. 3 below.) On a blank sheet of paper the same size, trace around the puzzle pieces as they should appear in finished form. Place adhesive backing on the puzzle pieces. Allow one or two children to put the puzzle together in front of the group. Discuss the meaning of the verse. Have children repeat the verse in unison three or four times.

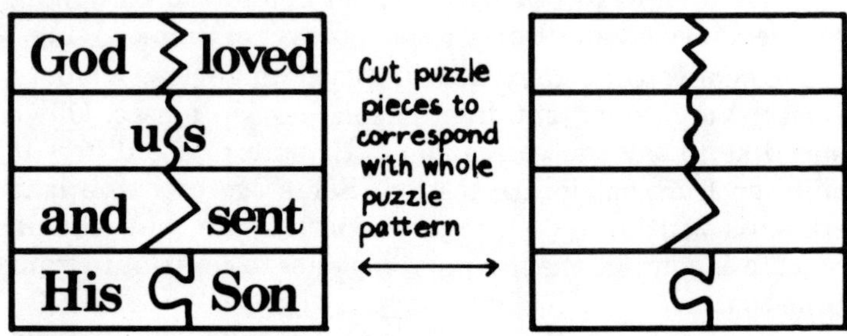

b. Missing letters. On poster board, or a large sheet of paper, print a scripture reference and the verse to be learned, leaving out several letters. Ask children to

F__ __ G__d s__
lo__ed t__ __ wo__l__
t__a__ __ __ g__v__
H__ __ on__ __
b__go__ __en __ __ __ __.

John 3:16

34

assist you in looking up the verse and filling in the missing letters. This is especially useful with short or familiar verses.

    c. Scroll. Use a long, narrow strip of paper and dowels or unsharpened pencils to make a scroll. Print the verse on the scroll. This is especially appropriate when studying the teachings of Jesus and Moses. A discussion about scrolls increases student understanding of the original manuscripts, which looked so unlike our books.

    d. Echo. The teacher says a verse which has been written on a large sheet of paper. The class repeats the verse with the teacher. Children continue repeating the verse, saying it softer each time until they whisper it the last time.

    e. Putting in order. When a verse relates to a story with an easily illustrated object, cut out outlines of that object. Write one word of the verse on each object. Students place the words in order. For the story of the loaves and fishes, for example, the verse may be written on paper fish.

Or write the words on pieces of cardboard cut out like loaves of bread. Place the loaves in a basket, then have the children pull out the words and put them in order.

Many of the memory verse objects can be used later in the scripture center to reinforce all the verses of the unit.

Whatever method of presentation is used, repeat the verse enough times for the children to commit it to memory. One time through is never enough; but repetition alone is boring, so use a variety of techniques. Review memory verses in the opening of the next session, and/or at a closing time group meeting after interest center activities have been completed.

Recognizing birthdays and visitors during the opening by name draws them to the attention of regular attenders. If your group meets only during the school year, as some Caravans do, recognize summer birthdays at a meeting near the end of the term. Some teachers designate these times as UNbirthday sessions. Singing the traditional birthday song usually suffices for recognition of this special day in the child's life.

5. Interest Centers

After all preliminaries have been taken care of, the children may go to interest centers.

There are three main methods of interest center selection. First, for nursery-aged children, and in churches where the number of centers must be limited to two or three activity areas per session, it is advisable to divide the group into nearly equal numbers at each center. Each small group goes to a center, the activity is performed in a set time (15 to 25 minutes, depending on the activity and the total time available), a signal is given, and the groups move to another center. During the session, each group has ample opportunity to experience each center.

The second method of center selection allows more freedom and may be used with children of primary age or older when there is a larger number of centers. Children are dismissed from the opening by small groups to go to the activity of their choice, until the maximum number for a center is reached. As in the first method, when a signal is given, the child moves to another center. In this setup, the child must choose which centers he wishes to explore. He cannot attend them all.

The third method allows for the most flexibility and is best used after the children have become accustomed to the increased freedom of movement in the interest center environment. This method assumes that when given the choice, children will select centers that interest them, and learn better because of that interest.

Before making choices, children may be led through the entire room to survey what activities are available. This helps them to make choices of which they feel more sure, thus preventing trial-and-failure or disinterest at the center. However, there are some positive guidelines to use in helping the children select centers.

a. Allow the youngest to choose first when there is a wide age span among the group.

b. Some centers have a maximum student limit. A child may come to that center when a chair becomes empty, as long as there is time to complete the project.

c. A child may spend as much or as little time as he desires at a center.

If there is a favorite center, offer it for as many sessions as necessary to meet the interests of the group. Younger children, especially, will feel more secure to see the same materials, such as a dress-up or block center, time after time.

In this third kind of selection process, dismiss children from the opening by grade, by those wearing a particular color, by those wearing short sleeves, or by birthday months. This provides impartial dismissal, yet allows small groups to go instead of everyone going to the same place at the same time.

Remember, behavior during centers time will vary from the traditional classroom conduct. The noise level at first will be frightening to some adults. Firmness and consistent gentle reminders to use soft voices and slow feet will eventually bring a quieter atmosphere. However, there will always be *some* talking and *some* movement. That is to be expected, but it can be controlled. The calm, gentle actions of the teachers will do much in leading the children to maintain order.

6. Cleanup

Children should clean their work areas as they complete an activity. Near the end of center time, all should be involved in putting away materials. Of course, the age and abilities of the children must be considered in the amount of detail expected in cleanup time.

7. Wrap-up

Call the children back to the large-group setting used in the opening for 5 or 10 minutes before dismissal time. This provides opportunity for communication between total staff and students. It is also an excellent place to reinforce the concepts taught that day, or it may be used as a time of worship. A few teachers may quietly finish cleanup tasks, especially if another group is to use the room later.

SAMPLE PROCEDURE FOR OLDER CHILDREN
(Grades 4 through 6)

In church programs designed for children in the upper elementary grades, the procedure will have different emphases than that used with early elementary students.

For instance, self-consciousness and peer pressure become evident in the large group setting with these older pupils. These characteristics have less influence on most groups of younger children.

Fourth, fifth, and sixth grade pupils may hesitate to participate in worship activities, even when the task requires only general knowledge that almost everyone possesses. These preteens often seem embarrassed when singled out; they do not want to be known as "show-offs." They may even refuse to suggest a favorite song. Finding his place in the group is more important than the student's need of individual recognition. The youngest of this age range are especially insecure while they are trying to determine what the larger group expects of them.

With the approach of puberty, moods may change drastically from week to week. Remember that this is just human development. Remind teachers that these switches are not their fault. The motto "This, too, shall pass" should be etched on the workers' hearts as they portray Christ's love to these moody ones.

Though the large group function may differ from that of the younger group, the one-to-one teacher-to-child relationship remains just as important—maybe more so. In fact, since uncertainty marks much of the junior's relationships, he needs reassurance of his individual worth. Meeting this need should have high priority in the teacher-pupil association for children in these grades.

Because of the difference between younger and older children, the leader may wish to use one of the following scheduling arrangements.

1. Split Session

Divide the children into two groups of approximately equal numbers. One group attends a story time or a Bible study time. The other group goes to centers—two or three centers per session. The two groups switch activities at the midway point of the meeting.

Advantages to this alternative are that all the students are exposed to the teaching objective for the day, and teachers have only one preparation for two presentations. Also, during center time students have a choice of activities according to individual interests.

2. Children's Choice

This method gives the students an even larger range of choices. The room is set up completely with centers, the number depending on the size of the group. Seven to 10 children per adult is a workable number. This method is used most effectively with a small, responsible group of eager learners. Larger groups may experience some difficulty with it because of peer pressure and self-consciousness. Since individuals are eager to please the group, attendance at some centers may be sparse and at others nearly overwhelming. If a student who is recognized as a leader by the group exhibits irresponsible behavior—showing disinterest, inability to decide on a center, or failure to complete a task—his attitudes can quickly encompass others in the group, and little learning will be achieved.

To encourage meaningful involvement at the centers, small incentive plans have been employed successfully by some teachers. Previously unmotivated students often will work for a tangible reward. Requirements may be simple, such as completing two center projects to earn one certificate. Certificates are assigned a predetermined value and are exchanged for the wanted item. Many inexpensive items with a spiritual emphasis can be obtained from your publishing house and/or from a local Christian bookstore. If you work with a weekday program, it is advisable to set the requirements so that it is necessary for the child to earn certificates by the end of three or four weeks, or at the end of a unit.

Another incentive is to let the child go to the craft center after completing the workbook or Bible game center activities.

3. Center a Session

This method of scheduling has been used effectively when the number of workers is small and the group is large.

Divide the group into grade levels. The number of centers set up correspond to the number of grade levels. Students of one grade level go to one center per session, then rotate at the next sessions until all grade levels have attended each center. The advantage to this is that the teacher has only one preparation, adapted, of course, to the needs of the students in each grade level. The disadvantage is that each center must contain enough material to interest and occupy the student for the whole session time.

4. Centers—Group—Centers

This method works well when group tardiness is a problem. Set up the more fun-centered activities, such as crafts, filmstrips, and Bible games, for use during the first 25 minutes of a one-hour meeting. Then call the large group together for worship for about 10 minutes. After this, groups go to centers of a more serious nature—a story center, a workbook center, a research center—for the remaining time.

This arrangement combines both old and new teaching methods. Also, students leave the classroom on a serious note and with the day's learning fresh in their minds. In addition, it provides opportunity to use in one part of the program personnel who hesitate to be involved in the total program.

5. Opening, Then to Centers

Many of the ideas found in the suggested schedule for early elementary students are also found in this method of scheduling. The program session is opened with a full-group activity, followed by center time. The time allotted for opening depends on the nature of the group. A restless group may need the structure the opening provides to calm their behavior.

Here are some additional ideas to keep in mind:

a. Avoid embarrassing a child by drawing attention to him unless he feels comfortable in participating.

b. Have a presession activity center available for early arrivers, such as a notebook project which can be added to as work is completed. Consult the Sunday school resource packets for ideas for this center, even if you are formulating centers for another program.

c. Learn to exercise a "third ear." Remember that the students will not always say what they really mean. For instance, "No, I do not want to pray in opening," may mean "If I could be sure that my friends would support me, I would enjoy praying during opening." Also, some will be noticeably verbal (some mothers call it "mouthy") to attract attention to themselves.

d. Some older ones in the group may tend to be critical of procedures and/or activities. It is helpful to use the children in the evaluative process at the end of a quarter or unit; but because of this tendency toward a negative attitude in some of them, it is wise to approach the evaluators individually.

e. Avoid questions that can be answered with a yes or no. Use queries that require a positive statement of preference instead of giving the child a chance to focus on dislikes. Instead of asking, "Did you like this center?" ask, "Which centers would you like to see repeated with different materials?" Or, "Is there a center we haven't done for a while that you prefer?"

f. To reduce anxiety about participation, some junior leaders have found that preteens more willingly say the offertory prayer during opening than the devotional prayer. It is advisable to consult with the child and get his consent before calling on him. One public refusal is like a disease; others then will refuse, too.

g. Using student ushers to pass offering plates provides excellent training for the adult worship service.

h. If children agree to share testimonies of what Christ means to them, opening is an opportune time for witnessing. If there is hesitancy or refusal, plan for the teachers to occasionally share a short, lively testimony about some way Christ helps them. Some children are involved in only one program of the church, and this may be the only witnessing they hear. Sunday school workers especially should be aware of this possibility. Such testimonies also focus attention on the spiritual reason why the group is assembled in the church setting. Eventually, we hope to see each child serving Christ as a responsible adult.

i. Older elementary children sing most enthusiastically when using more difficult songs such as rounds, those with unusual rhythm, or even tongue-twisting lyrics. On the other hand, younger children sing best when the song is familiar.

j. The large group setting is ideal for review of story elements, unit theme, or program objectives.

k. Birthdays are still important to these children, but sing the traditional song only if an individual seems comfortable with that much singing out. Otherwise just mention the name and give a small gift.

l. When using the children's choice of centers described earlier, groups may be efficiently dismissed by interest. For the other setups, group assignments may be announced during opening.

m. Older elementary students should play a more dependable role in cleanup of the center area, so the wrap-up group activity may be omitted or used only occasionally.

Specific center ideas are given in Chapters 4 and 5. Though teachers will not want to provide only difficult tasks, middler- and junior-aged children respond better to challenge than to pleasure and fun, so characteristic of nursery and early elementary learning. And this is a challenge for the teacher, too!

Chapter 4

Centers to Begin With

How many centers should one start a program with? To decide this, consider the number in the department, or program, and the number of teachers available. The ratio of teachers to students should be no more than 1:10. The fewer students at a center, the more individual attention the teacher will be able to give. Age of the students is also a factor. Preschool centers should probably have a ratio of 1:5.

Experience shows that centers which can accommodate 10 children will operate more smoothly with less than 10. With 20 to 30 older children, three to four centers will be adequate. If the department has room, more centers could be set up and the children even further divided.

For groups of seven or more, an assistant, in addition to the teacher, helps the center operate more smoothly.

One caution should be given before beginning: Be prepared for an occasional unexpected failure for a center which the adults thought the children would enjoy—and unexpected success for a center which the adults thought rather uninteresting. The failure may have nothing to do with any person's ability or lack of it, so avoid disappointment by simply accepting the rejection of the center and removing it from use for following sessions. For the unexpected successes, honor the children's interest by offering the center often until participation wanes.

Centers used in the beginning of a new program should be few and simple. This will enable both teachers and children to become accustomed gradually to the new procedure.

Following are several simple center ideas with which to begin a learning center. Note the suggested grade levels, the materials needed, instructions for the student, the teacher's role, and the possible themes for correlating the activity to the learned concept. Suggested grade levels are not absolute; consider the needs and abilities of each group in determining usability of a center idea.

In reading Chapters 4 and 5, remember that these ideas are intended to encourage creativity on the part of the teachers in a learning center program. Many specific directions are suggested, but other curriculum resources can be utilized to provide meaningful activities in the centers.

Center: **Story**

Suggested Grade Levels: **Nursery** through junior. This center is imperative unless the story is done for the total group at one time.

Materials Needed: **A** story applicable to the unit theme, and visual aids, such as *Nu-Vu* or objects to illustrate things in the story. Visual aids are crucial in impressing the story upon the minds of the hearers. Puppets may be used to introduce the story; or they may help tell the story by engaging in dialogue either with the storyteller or between two puppets. Young children may sit on an area rug; older children may prefer comfortable chairs, arranged in a semicircle around the storyteller.

Student Task: Listen; participate verbally when requested. Sometimes the story center can also be used as a review center where small groups of students retell the story they heard earlier. Volunteers may retell the story, one idea at a time; or several may tell the whole story, if time and interest permit.

Teacher's Role: The adult in this center should have a knack for telling stories with good voice expression, should be able to control a group, should be confident of himself before groups of young listeners, should study the story so diligently that little reading will be necessary during the actual presentation, and should display patience with interruptions when telling a story to young listeners. A person with these skills will captivate the audience and will be free to use visual aids in presenting the story.

Possible Use with Unit Themes: Stories may be found to support almost any theme being taught.

Center: **Workbook, or activity book**

Suggested Grade Levels: Nursery through junior

Materials Needed: Curriculum workbook or activity book. Check each session for additional materials needed. The teacher's manual will contain explicit directions on how to use the workbook.

Student Task: Student, sitting in group around a table, will complete the activity as directed in the teacher's manual.

Teacher's Role: Provide the materials specified in the teacher's manual, and guide children in completing the activity. This center is especially adaptable for

teachers and students who function best with structured activity. The center may be combined with the story center in middler and junior groups, if the curriculum story is not told in an opening or large-group setting.

Possible Use with Unit Themes: Use with all themes, whenever curriculum materials provide workbook activities.

Center: **Memory**

Suggested Grade Levels: Kindergarten through junior

Materials Needed: Various games; incentives to encourage memorization of scripture related to current learnings

Student Task: Memorize verse(s) of the session or unit.

Teacher's Role: Provide meaningful materials to encourage scripture memorization. Here are a few ideas:

1. "Lollipops for Learning." The teacher may write a series of verses, such as the Ten Command-

ments, one each, on round pieces of poster board. Securely attach a flat stick to the back of each with masking tape. The student may select a candy lollipop after he can successfully recite a certain number of verses in order. Remember to make the goals attainable. Each child may take his own set of cardboard lollipops home after memorizing the entire set.

2. Middlers and juniors enjoy pairing off and challenging one another in learning verses. "Match Verses," "Bible Verse Flip," "Match the Halves," and "Take Ten" are only a few of the many games suggested in *Let's Teach with Bible Games,* by Donna Fillmore. Use these games to teach, reinforce, and review Bible verses at the memory center.

3. "Fishing." Make a pattern of a fish. Cut out 24 fish from blue construction paper or plain file cards. Put the scripture on one fish, where it is found on another. Continue the same way with 12 verses. Attach a paper clip to each fish. Use a dowel for

a fishing pole, with a small horseshoe magnet tied to the end. The child fishes and tries to match verses and references. Having a partner for challenge to see who gets the most matches adds interest. (This activity should be self-checking. Use symbols such as a ✔ on one matched set, * on another, & on another, and so on.)

4. "Mini-Puzzles." Use a small plain file card or colorful tagboard. Print a memory verse on each card, then cut apart into puzzle pieces. Store each puzzle in a separate letter-sized envelope.

5. "Strawberry Box." Use a strawberry pattern, or anything seasonal, and cut out several berry shapes. Cut the tops separately. Print the Bible verse to be learned on a strawberry, with its reference on the stem. Put the same mark on backs of matching berries and stems to make this a self-checking activity. Place all pieces in a commercial quart strawberry box.

Possible Use with Unit Themes: Bible memorization is vital to any religious education program. The memory center should be a permanent one. However, the teacher in charge should be alert to the need for changing the activities so the children's interest will be sustained in the center.

Center: Book corner

Suggested Grade Levels: Nursery through junior

Materials Needed: Book rack, or low table with four to six suitable chairs; area rug, carpet squares, or short stools; assorted books with religious emphasis

Student Task: Read, or listen to helper read book that student selects.

Teacher's Role: Stimulate conversation regarding the reading materials. Help child select books, if he de-

sires help. Read to nonreading students. Be familiar with most of the books in order to encourage readers.

The book corner may be varied occasionally by displaying only books dealing with the unit theme. Short books may be recorded on cassette tape so the child may listen to the tape as he follows in the book.

An incentive program may be set up to encourage reading. A cloth bag of inexpensive surprises is useful with young readers. "Reach in for your gift after each story," will add excitement to the book corner with the surprise bag. A goal-oriented incentive may be used to increase motivation for older students.

A check-out system may be used if an ample supply of books is available.

Possible Use with Unit Themes: Books can complement all unit themes.

Center: **Listening**
Suggested Grade Levels: Nursery through junior

Materials Needed: Record player; four to six sets of earphones (if possible); appropriate records, cassette tape recorders, book-tape combinations, and blank tapes for student use

Student Task: Younger children will enjoy listening to taped stories or singing along with musical records. They will need assistance in operating the electrical equipment. Older elementary children may learn to operate the various media, letting them learn or reinforce lesson principles of the day through listening on their own schedule.

Teacher's Role: Operation of equipment for young students; supervision and encouragement of responsible use of machines for older children. A teacher should be available to instruct in the proper use of machines and to help with any problems that may arise.

Possible Use with Unit Themes: This center is especially useful with holiday themes, for singing activities, or in teaching new songs. Book listening is adaptable to all themes.

The listening center may be easily converted into a music center. Preschoolers enjoy experimenting with various rhythm instruments. Early elementary children may make and use crude replicas of biblical musical instruments. Juniors can research how Bible instruments are related to modern ones.

In a unit on reaching out to care for others, or with Bible stories of Jesus healing the deaf, the listening center can be used for discussion of deafness and its related problems.

Juniors may use the listening center to make tapes for preschool and early elementary students to listen to. The young child may wish to follow alone in the book as he listens. Thus, the listening center may serve also as a service center.

Center: **Games**

Suggested Grade Levels: Primary; middler; junior

Materials Needed: Assorted Bible games. Bible facts can be made into a variety of interesting, challenging games. See Donna Fillmore's book, *Let's Teach with Bible Games,* for excellent ideas and explicit, easy-to-follow instructions. Also, check the Sunday school resource packets for game suggestions to be used with each unit. These games can often be adapted for use with other units, and even in programs other than Sunday school.

Student Task: Master the knowledge through participation in the game.

Teacher's Role: The teacher must know how to play the game, or games, used in the center so he can explain clearly the rules and method of playing. He

should help the students begin the game(s), then allow them to take over if they wish.

An incentive of some type may be provided for mastery of the knowledge required to successfully play each game. Since games differ widely, be sure to set up meaningful goals for each one.

The game center may be used also as a reward in itself. Let students go to this center when they complete activities that require more concentration and work, such as the memory center and workbook center.

Possible Use with Unit Themes: Bible games are especially appropriate for any kind of learning that is factual or which deals with chronology.

Suggested Games:

1. "Noah's Ark." Cover a box with adhesive paper. Put a hole in each end large enough for a child's hand to reach into the box. Place one set of miniature plastic animals inside box. Have another

set to place, one at a time, on top of the box. Have two children feel inside the box to see who can pull out the mate first.

2. "Wheel of Learning." Cut a circle with a 12" diameter out of poster board. Draw a circle in the middle and six spokes to look like an old wagon wheel. Cut out a window at the top and one at the bottom of the wheel, leaving one side of the windows attached so the flaps can be lifted to see inside. Cut out a 12" plain circle. Fasten the two wheels together with a paper fastener. Write on bottom wheel so that as it is rotated, questions appear at the bottom opening and the correct answer in the window at the top. Make a wheel for each lesson emphasis.

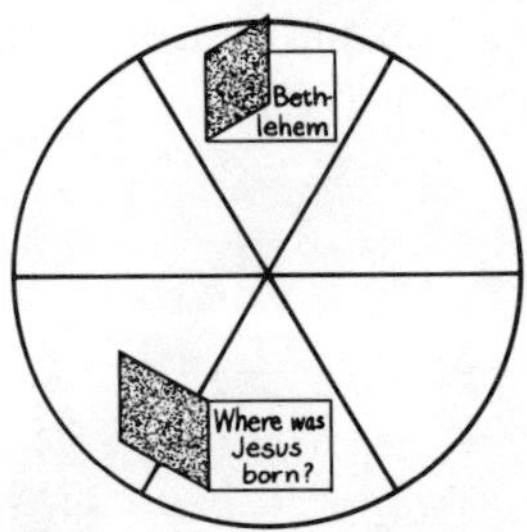

3. "Easter Eggs." Cut out egg shapes from poster board, making three or four eggs from each color. Cut each egg into two parts, using different jagged

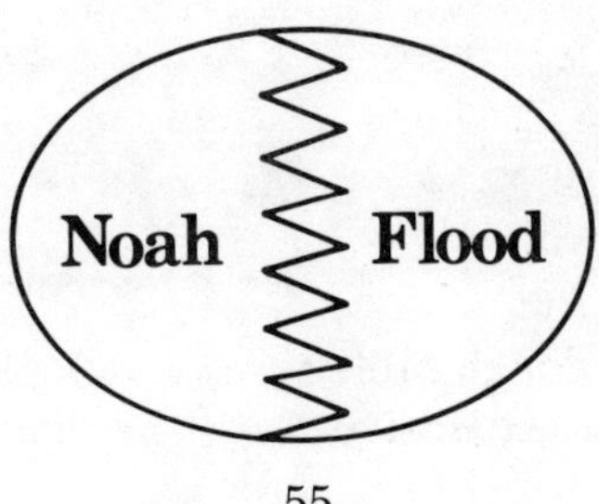

lines. Write an incident on one half of the egg, the answer on the other. Children match questions and answers by putting the two parts of each egg together.

Center: **Arts and crafts**

Suggested Grade Levels: Nursery through junior

Materials Needed: Those required by the specific craft. See "Student Task."

Student Task:

1. Easel center (preschool through young middlers). Provide an easel with manila paper and crayons, or smooth paper and tempera paints, for free expression of art. Narrow-necked soft-drink bottles aid in wiping excess paint from brushes as they are removed from the bottles.

2. Play dough table (preschool). Homemade play dough is less expensive than the commercial kinds,

and it can be colored with a small amount of food coloring to go along with the seasons. Play dough meets the need for manipulative materials for nursery-aged youngsters.

3. Collage center (nursery through junior). For preschool and kindergarten children, provide pictures already cut out of magazines. These should relate to the session or unit theme. Let children paste pictures randomly on pieces of construction paper. Older children can scan the magazines to find and cut out their own pictures.

Juniors may bring in related objects to add to their collages. For instance, for a collage about church a child may bring in a sheet of church stationery, a postcard with the church's picture, pictures of the staff, and so on. Middlers and juniors should be able to work in a group on a large collage.

4. Diorama (middler and junior). Older elementary children may enjoy working singly or in pairs to create a diorama illustrating some story or biblical event they have studied. Use the long side of the bottom portion of a shoe box as the base for the scene of the diorama. Students use various art media to create a three-dimensional scene.

5. "Big art" center (preschool and primary). Have the child lie down on butcher paper or newsprint. Draw an outline around the child. Cut it out for very young children; older ones may cut their own outlines. Children color their "self" image with crayons, decorating it however they wish. Tape paper children on walls around room, hands joining one another.

This idea stimulates conversation when studying units on accepting self, loving others as self, and growing up.

Middlers and juniors can participate in "big art"

by doing murals which depict the theme of a session or unit.

Teacher's Role and Possible Use with Unit Themes: These are described above.

Center: **Housekeeping**

Suggested Grade Levels: Nursery; kindergarten

Materials Needed: Play sink, stove, refrigerator, ironing board, iron, old throw rug, plastic or metal doll dishes, pans, doll bed; dolls. Group materials in a small area to simulate a room. If possible, place the dress-up center nearby.

Student Task: Act out feelings relating to self and/or family relationships. May simply enjoy pretending, an important way for young children to learn. Also, this area provides relief from work-oriented centers.

Teacher's Role: This center is self-motivating and self-sustaining so it requires little supervision. Teacher

may wish to provide a small amount of sudsy, warm water for ambitious dishwashers; splashed water is easily wiped up.

Possible Use with Unit Themes: Families; study of him/her self; sharing God's love in helping others.

Center: **Dress up**

Suggested Grade Levels: Nursery, kindergarten

Materials Needed: Clothes rack with reachable hooks; shelves; old clothes and shoes; strips of cloth that can be wrapped to look like Bible-time clothing; fake beards and wigs; mirror

Student Task: Try on clothing for pretending in the housekeeping center, or dress up like persons in Bible days.

Teacher's Role: Assist child in putting on garments, if child desires help. There need not be a full-time helper at this center, however. The teacher should comment on attractive garb and otherwise show appreciation for the child's efforts without embarrassing him.

Possible Use with Unit Themes: God plans for clothing; families. This center can be used also as a drama center in which pupils dress up and act out Bible stories. Have a teacher tell the story while another adult guides the children through a rough outline of the action involved. Seeing the story portrayed by characters in their own age-group helps to bring the story down to the children's level.

Center: Block corner

Suggested Grade Levels: Nursery; kindergarten

Materials Needed: Assorted sizes of wooden blocks. Large, sturdy building blocks may be made by taping down the pouring ends of empty half-gallon milk containers.

Student Task: Build structures related to the story theme,

such as the stable where Baby Jesus was born; or use in free play.

Large muscle coordination is developing at these ages, and children need opportunities to exercise without adult intervention. Children should help put blocks away when center time is finished.

Teacher's Role: May suggest that the child build a specific structure, as mentioned above. Usually, however, the teacher unobtrusively observes, ready to assist in problems of hoarding and so on. At end of session, the teacher assists in block pickup. A good rule for the block corner is that a child knocks down only what he has helped to build.

Possible Use with Unit Themes: Learning about Jesus' birthplace; units on the home and family. This center will probably be used most often for free play.

Chapter **5**

More, *More,* MORE Centers

The center ideas suggested in Chapter 4 are easy to begin with. The activities suggested in this chapter are offered for variety, and for use in churches with adequate space and the personnel to plan and supervise them.

If you put every center idea into operation, you will have ideas to last for many months. Centers are almost always used for more than one session before they are dismantled and rotated with other ideas. Too, a center may be used again with a ,later unit.

Center: **Puzzles**

Suggested Grade Levels: Nursery; kindergarten

Materials Needed: Simple, wooden-inlaid puzzles for pre-schoolers; more complicated ones with interlocking parts for older children

Student Task: Learn about his world by working puzzles with a variety of subjects.

Teacher's Role: Assist only when child is frustrated with his inability to put the puzzle together.

Possible Use with Unit Themes: Check your publishing house catalog for puzzles that relate to people, animals, and objects that the young child needs to learn about early in his religious education.

This center may be used also as a service project for middlers and juniors. Securely glue a teaching picture from the nursery or kindergarten curriculum onto a piece of poster board. Let dry thoroughly. Draw large puzzle pieces on the back of the poster board. Carefully cut out pieces. Present to Nursery or Kindergarten departments for the puzzle collection.

Center: Nu-Vu

Suggested Grade Levels: Nursery; kindergarten; primary

Materials Needed: Nu-Vu magnetic board and magnetic strips, obtainable from your publishing house; backgrounds and cutout figures used to illustrate Bible stories, available from the Sunday school resource packet.

Student Task: After the large group has heard the story and center groups are meeting, interested children

may use the figures to recreate the story for themselves.

Teacher's Role: Stay by *Nu-Vu* board for a few minutes to retell parts of the story to children. Suggest that the children move the figures about however they wish to review the story, or portions of it that they enjoyed most. If the children respond to such dialogue, the teacher may continue. However, if children want to play with the story figures alone, allow them to do so.

Possible Use with Unit Themes: Bible stories can be effectively reinforced in this way.

A flannelgraph board may be used in this same way. Simply cover a firm backing with plain-colored flannel. Paste flannel on back of story figure to make it adhere to the board. For younger children, cut outline figures from muslin. Little fingers cannot damage such materials.

Center: Filmstrip room

Suggested Grade Levels: Primary; middler; junior

Materials Needed: Filmstrip projector; electrical outlet; darkened room; screen or light-colored wall; appropriate filmstrips

Student Task: Young students will need supervision in setting up the equipment, but they enjoy turning the filmstrip once it is in the machine. Older students can thread the machine and operate it themselves. Some filmstrip models are automatic.

Teacher's Role: Stimulate and guide discussion of the filmstrip after it is shown.

Possible Use with Unit Themes: Purchase filmstrips that complement unit themes. Check your publishing house catalog for a listing of available filmstrips for purchase. You will also find projectors in a wide range

of prices. Such an investment will reap a bountiful harvest in reinforced learnings for many interested youngsters.

Center: Bulletin board

Suggested Grade Levels: Primary; middler; junior

Materials Needed: Art media, including construction paper; crepe paper; thumbtacks or staples; scissors; student work samples

Student Task: Plan and prepare a bulletin board to carry out the unit theme. Students should make a commitment to stay with the project until completion.

Teacher's Role: Provide ideas and assistance for younger students. Older students can complete the task with less adult help.

Possible Use with Unit Themes: Bulletin boards are easily correlated to any theme, or they can focus on a seasonal emphasis. Change the bulletin board with a seasonal theme for each unit. Monthly changes are ideal for boards.

Center: **Puppets**

Suggested Grade Levels: Nursery through middler

Materials Needed: Lunch-sized paper bags; construction paper; white glue or paste; scissors; bits of yarn; felt; ball fringe; washcloths; fine paintbrushes; plain-colored paper plates; wooden spoons; felt-tip markers; buttons; needles; tempera paints; thread

Student Task: Make various types of puppets from lunch bags, washcloths, paper plates, and wooden spoons.

Teacher's Role: Assist as needed in the puppet-making. Direct story review as suggested below.

Possible Use with Unit Themes: After constructing the puppets, the center can be used for review and reinforcement of the day's lesson. Puppets are especially useful in acting out Bible stories.

Juniors may wish to make more elaborate puppets, plan a puppet program around a story they have studied, and present the program to a younger department.

Center: **Nature**

Suggested Grade Levels: Nursery through junior

Materials Needed: Depends on the season and the kind of activity.

Student Task: Develop appreciation of God's created world through exploration of nature.

Teacher's Role: Encourage awareness of the bountiful and beautiful environment God has created for us to enjoy. Plan and supervise activity as necessary.

Possible Use with Unit Themes: This center is especially useful in studying the story of creation. It may be used also in discussing our stewardship of natural resources.

A few seasonal ideas include:

Spring

Discuss new plant life; plant seeds, watch them sprout and grow; experiment with proper and improper watering and lighting. Older students may discuss these principles in relation to people and the development of attitudes in response to kind vs. unkind treatment.

1. To plant seeds, place potting soil in separate sections of an empty egg carton. Plant different kinds of seeds in each section (orange, grapefruit, lemon, pumpkin, assorted flower seeds) and observe differences in foliage, rate of growth, response to light, and so on. Pupils may wish to transplant seedlings into pots after a few weeks.

2. Line a quart jar with a wet paper towel, then

fill jar with sand. Place lima beans between the towel and side of the jar, so they can be seen from the outside. Add water as needed to keep towel moist. Keep in sunny spot. Observe the sprouting and rooting process.

Summer

1. Suggest that children bring in smooth rocks from their vacations for rock painting. Use tempera paints for this activity. They may also enjoy gluing rocks together to form rock sculpture.

2. Encourage children to bring bouquets of fresh garden flowers to brighten the room.

Fall

1. Coat leaves with tempera paint. Turn painted side of leaf onto light-colored or white construction paper to make a leaf impression. Remove leaf. Use different colors of paint to heighten the attractiveness of the picture.

2. Place a pad of newspaper on a flat surface.

On this, place a layer of waxed paper; then leaves to be waxed; and last, another piece of waxed paper and a single thickness of newspaper. With adult supervision let children iron until heat transfers wax onto the leaves. Use leaves on bulletin boards, in centerpieces, or in art pictures. They can be stored and used again, if desired.

3. Using the process described above, scatter crayon shavings between leaves. Young children can shave with plastic knives. Make frame for this wax picture by cutting out the center of a piece of 9 x 12 autumn-colored construction paper, leaving a 1½-inch to 2-inch border. Attach waxed picture to frame. Place piece of yarn in punched-out holes at top of frame and display in window.

4. To make leaf silhouettes, place leaves in a design on manila or white drawing paper. Rub colored chalk in a small area on fine sandpaper, a chalkboard, or a separate sheet of paper. Use facial tissue to rub chalk powder on paper, with strokes going away from the leaf to leave a shadowy, feathery effect. Remove leaf and the silhouette remains.

Winter

1. Provide white chalk and dark-colored or black construction paper for making snow pictures.

2. Feature white paint and dark paper at the easel for painting snow scenes.

3. In northern states discuss the scarcity of natural bird food dispensers. In warmer climates, display fruit that is produced in these cooler months. Even though temperature changes are not always drastic in all areas of the country, the growing cycle provided by God's plan can be pointed out and observed by the children.

Center: **Service**

Suggested Grade Levels: Middler; junior

Materials Needed: As required by the project selected

1. Stationery center. Cut colored or white Ditto paper in half and fold to make notepaper. Let students decorate one side of the note. They may write a short note to absentees, to a shut-in, or a note of appreciation to their parents. Pupils may also make up collections of decorated notepaper to wrap and give to elderly invalids of the church at Christmastime or for birthday gifts.

2. A child, or children, may dictate that session's story to an adult. Center activity involves making the story into a book that can be read by, or to, students who have been absent.

3. Practice songs to sing to shut-ins, or to use in a visitation program to absentees.

4. Bring in money, canned goods, mittens, or

other items to give to someone in need. This is an especially good project at Thanksgiving or Christmas.

5. The cooking center, listening center, creative writing center, puppet center, holiday center, and puzzle center may all be used for service projects. Ideas are given in the discussion of each center.

Possible Use with Unit Themes: These projects are especially applicable to discipleship units which teach the child to care for and share with others.

Center: Creative writing

Suggested Grade Levels: Primary; middler; junior

Materials Needed: Lined paper for story or poem(s); construction paper, wallpaper samples, or poster board for book covers; heavy-duty stapler, or yarn and darning needles to bind books

Student Task: Make a blank book to fill in with one of the following possibilities:

1. Write original endings to situation stories (read by the teacher) which relate to the unit theme.

2. Record the possible feelings expressed in pictures displayed by the teacher.

3. Older students may write an entire story on some aspect of interpersonal discipleship, when studying such a unit.

4. Juniors may use the books as a log of their own feelings, or of personal progress in areas of interpersonal or peer-group discipleship. Teachers should read only the books that students are willing to share. This activity can heighten the child's awareness of appropriate behavior in relating to others.

Teacher's Role: The teacher will play an active role in the young students' participation in this center. These children may dictate what they want in their books,

and the teacher will write it for them. For all ages
the teacher provides constant encouragement but is
careful not to hamper creativity. A beautiful book is
not as important as a meaningful one.

Children who desire may illustrate their books.
The younger child may wish to read his book to the
entire group upon completion of the project.

Remember to plan the length and degree of involvement in such an activity by the ability and skill
levels of average individuals in the age-group. A
second grader will not have the attention span of a
sixth grader, nor will his product be as complex.

Possible Use with Unit Themes: This center is especially
adaptable to units on self. However, students may
also write about their church and discipleship as mentioned above.

The creative writing center may also be used to
make books for the Nursery Department. Middlers
and juniors can sew cloth pages together in book form
to make "See, Touch, and Do" books. A bright picture of an animal, a cotton ball or a piece of velvet
to touch, a zipper to work—these are just a few ideas
for such a book. Such books also make fitting "Baby
Day" gifts.

Center: **Holiday**

Suggested Grade Levels: Nursery through junior

Student Task: Learn about religious and other holidays.

Teacher's Role: Plan activities with pupils and supervise
as necessary.

Some secular holidays can be adapted to religious
uses. For instance, near Valentine's Day, one junior
leader provided construction paper and decorative
media for making valentines for themselves at the

center. Preceding this activity, the group discussed
Jesus' love for them. They then wrote a message to
themselves saying what they thought Jesus might say
to them if He were on earth in person today. Emphasis was placed upon scriptures relating to Jesus' love.

This center can also be set up to make cards or
small gifts on Christmas, Easter, Mother's Day,
Father's Day, and/or Grandparents' Day. Biblical
Jewish holidays and feasts can be researched by middlers and juniors. A study of the Christian sacraments
is one outgrowth of such an investigation.

Center: **Research**

Suggested Grade Levels: Middler; junior

Materials Needed: Bible with concordance; Bible dictionary; Bible encyclopedias; children's Bible story
collections; lined paper for recording findings; specific
assignments for information to look up; construction
paper to make folder to hold notes

Student Task: Learn to use Bible reference materials by
completing research project as outlined by the
teacher.

Teacher's Role: Compose questions that will challenge
pupils to look up little-known, but relevant, material
that enlarge upon the principles being learned. Encourage students and give guidance in using Bible
reference materials.

Possible Use with Unit Themes: This center can be used
effectively with students who enjoy an academic challenge. It is appropriate when studying Bible customs,
Bible history, and the lives of famous Bible persons.
It may also be used as a presession activity for early
arrivers.

The research center may be set up on a contract

basis, so that the project is designed in levels of accomplishment. The student decides how much he wishes to complete, signs his name to that commitment, and works toward that goal. There may be an award of some sort for the completion of each level. The award may be a tangible, inexpensive gift, or it may be the privilege to participate in a more fun-oriented center.

Center: **Plaster of Paris**

Suggested Grade Levels: Kindergarten; primary; middler

Materials Needed: Molded items; watercolors or felt-tip markers

Student Task: Paint a selected plaster of Paris item.

Teacher's Role: Inexpensive molds of durable, reusable plastic may be purchased at religious bookstores or at craft stores. Select small, easy-to-decorate styles for younger students. Purchase dry plaster of Paris at a craft store. Mix one part water to two parts dry

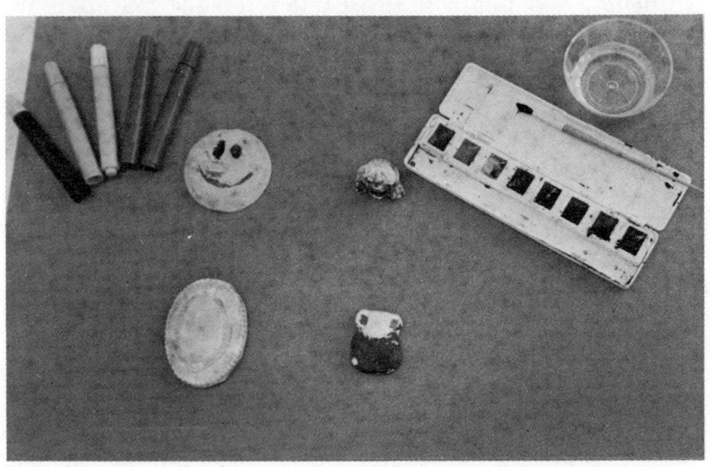

plaster of Paris. Prepare molded items in advance. Supervise students at the center as needed.

Possible Use with Unit Themes: This craft idea may be reserved for relaxation. It does not necessarily relate each session to a unit theme, but it may be used around holiday times for gift-making. Or it may be used for a service project to make cheery gifts for shut-ins.

Center: Cooking

Suggested Grade Levels: Nursery through middler

Materials Needed: As required by the project selected

Student Task, Teacher's Role: The teacher will do most of the work with younger children, but even the very youngest enjoy taking turns stirring. Older students may participate more in measuring and mixing according to the skills of their age-group.

Possible Use with Unit Themes: This center may be used for making and tasting Bible foods. This will be especially meaningful when the Bible story deals with food in some way, such as Jesus feeding the 5,000. Juniors may first do research into the diet and typical foods of biblical times.

Around holiday seasons, this center may be used to make baked food gifts for shut-ins.

Center: Woodworking

Suggested Grade Levels: Kindergarten through junior

Materials Needed: Scrap wood for younger children, easy wood projects for older ones; hammers; nails; saws; paints (if desired); glue; an old table to use as a workbench

This center functions well in a small classroom by itself. Remind concerned adults that these children

are not *working* as an adult carpenter would be; they are learning as they *play*.

Ask church members to donate scrap lumber they may have left over from home do-it-yourself projects. Lumber companies will sometimes donate scraps for nonprofit organizations. Ask builders in new home building areas for the discards from the rough carpentry.

Some person in the church who has an electric saw will be glad to cut the scrap lumber into the sizes desired—either uniform patterns for certain projects, or just into sizes that are manageable by the age-group using the center.

Student Task: Preschoolers enjoy gluing bits of scrap lumber onto a 12 x 12 piece of corrugated cardboard to make their own creation. Primary children enjoy sawing and gluing to make a simple object, such as a sailboat or an airplane. Middlers and juniors can make bird feeders or birdhouses from precut pieces.

Teacher's Role: Make sure that proper materials are prepared in advance and give assistance as needed. The person in charge of this center should be on the lookout for ideas for wood projects and should possess some ability in carpentry. This is an excellent center for men who don't want leadership roles in a program but who enjoy working with children.

Possible Use with Unit Themes: This center helps to bring meaning to the knowledge that Jesus was a carpenter and was raised in a carpenter's home. It also provides an outlet for students who tire of academic endeavors and more precise creative projects, such as small crafts and creative writing.

Chapter 6

Getting It All Together

"How will this method of teaching affect other children's ministries in the local church?" a children's ministries director may ask.

As mentioned earlier, the Sunday school is often the first department in a church to try the learning center approach. There are several reasons for this.

First, Sunday school is the time provided to concentrate on religious education. Adults and children alike meet for that hour. Since education is the prime purpose of the Sunday school program, many trained teachers volunteer to use their educational background in its teaching ranks. Since public education in recent years has been turning toward more individualized education, these teachers have adapted those concepts to religious education also.

Second, regardless of the size of the church, the Sunday school program is one of the first organizations formed. This means that every church could use the learning center approach, adapting it as necessary.

Third, wherever the learning center approach is begun, it may be correlated easily with all other existing children's ministries in a local church. The director of children's ministries of a local church may coordinate uses of centers from various programs, if desired. Leaders of the various children's organizations would meet monthly to decide what kinds of centers could best be shared by all groups. These centers can be set up and left for all groups to use. Centers to be used in only one program can be stored between sessions of that group.

Each local church's agenda for children's activities is different, so details will have to be worked out for the particular ministries involved. Loving cooperation of leaders is the key to successful coordination.

Ministering to interested, learning children is the goal of learning center education. With prayerful preparation and a staff dedicated to meet the needs of each student, learning centers can prove to be a blessing to Christian education. With that in mind, pray—then give interest centers a try. The open doors in such a children's ministry need never close.

Bibliography

BARTH, ROLAND S. *Open Education and the American School.* New York: Agathon Press, Inc., 1972.

BLITZ, BARBARA. *The Open Classroom: Making It Work.* Boston: Allyn and Bacon, Inc., 1972.

BUCKLEY, HELEN. "The Little Boy," *School Arts* magazine, October, 1961.

DUCKERT, MARY. *Open Education Goes to Church.* Philadelphia: Westminster Press, 1976.

FILLMORE, DONNA. *Let's Teach with Bible Games.* Kansas City: Beacon Hill Press of Kansas City, 1978.

KING, PAT HOPSON. *Games That Teach.* Encino, Calif.: International Center for Educational Development, 1971. (Good games resource book.)

LIPSCHITZ, CEIL. *An Ecology Craftbook for the Open Classroom.* New York: The Center for Applied Research in Education, Inc., 1975. (Good source book for easy crafts.)

SILBERMAN, CHARLES E., ed. *The Open Classroom Reader.* New York: Vintage Books, 1973.

SMITH, LEE L. *Jack out of the Box.* West Nyack, N.Y.: Parker Publishing Co., Inc., 1974.

THOMAS, JOHN I. *Learning Centers.* Boston: Holbrook Publishers, 1975.